SEASONS OF FUN: SPRING

SPRING HOLIDAYS

by J. P. Press

Consultant: Beth Gambro
Reading Specialist, Yorkville, Illinois

Minneapolis, Minnesota

Teaching Tips

Before Reading

- Look at the cover of the book. Discuss the picture and the title.
- Ask readers to brainstorm a list of what they already know about spring holidays. What can they expect to see in the book?
- Go on a picture walk, looking through the pictures to discuss vocabulary and make predictions about the text.

During Reading

- Read for purpose. Encourage readers to think about the special days in spring as they are reading.
- Ask readers to look for the details of the book. What is happening on these days?
- If readers encounter an unknown word, ask them to look at the sounds in the word. Then, ask them to look at the rest of the page. Are there any clues to help them understand?

After Reading

- Encourage readers to pick a buddy and reread the book together.
- Ask readers to name three spring holidays from the book. Go back and find the pages that tell about these things.
- Ask readers to write or draw something they learned about spring holidays.

Credits:
Cover and title page, © Bhupi/iStock, © aurora/iStock; 3, © skodonnell/iStock; 5, © Suzette Leg Anthony/Shutterstock; 6–7, © Soumen Hazra/Shutterstock; 9, © rblfmr/Shutterstock; 10, © Bernardo Emanuelle/Shutterstock; 12, © Alexandar Iotzov/Shutterstock; 13, © id-art/Shutterstock; 14, © dnaveh/Shutterstock; 15, © TinaFields/iStock; 16, © WIBOON WIRATTHANAPHAN/Shutterstock; 17, © Maples Images/Shutterstock; 18–19, © Light and Vision/Shutterstock; 20, © Svitlana Martynova/Shutterstock; 21, © omgimages/iStock; 22, © janrysavy/iStock, © Bettmann/gettyimages, © Claudiad/iStock, © David Pereiras/Shutterstock; 23TL, © Jean-Adolphe Beauce/Wikipedia; 23TM, © wundervisuals/iStock; 23TR, © Larina Marina/Shutterstock; 23BL, © Steve Edreff/Shutterstock; 23BM, © Nastco/iStock; 23BR, © tovfla/iStock.

Library of Congress Cataloging-in-Publication Data

Names: Press, J. P., 1993- author.
Title: Spring holidays / by J. P. Press ; Consultant : Beth Gambro, Reading
   Specialist, Yorkville, Illinois.
Description: Minneapolis, Minnesota : Bearport Publishing Company, 2022. |
   Series: Seasons of fun: spring | Includes bibliographical references and index.
Identifiers: LCCN 2021030921 (print) | LCCN 2021030922 (ebook) | ISBN
   9781636913957 (library binding) | ISBN 9781636914008 (paperback) | ISBN
   9781636914053 (ebook)
Subjects: LCSH: Holidays--Juvenile literature. | Spring--Juvenile literature.
Classification: LCC GT3933 .P74 2022 (print) | LCC GT3933 (ebook) | DDC
   394.26--dc23
LC record available at https://lccn.loc.gov/2021030921
LC ebook record available at https://lccn.loc.gov/2021030922

Copyright © 2022 Bearport Publishing Company. All rights reserved. No part of this publication may be reproduced in whole or in part, stored in a retrieval system, or transmitted in any form or by any means, electronic, mechanical, photocopying, recording, or otherwise, without written permission from the publisher.

For more information, write to Bearport Publishing, 5357 Penn Avenue South, Minneapolis, MN 55419. Printed in the United States of America.

Contents

Holiday Fun 4

The Story of Earth Day 22

Glossary 23

Index 24

Read More 24

Learn More Online 24

About the Author 24

Holiday Fun

It is time for spring fun!

There are many fun days in the spring.

Some of them are holidays.

I love spring holidays!

Holi is a holiday to welcome spring.

It started in India.

But now it is all over the world.

People throw colored dust at each other.

On St. Patrick's Day, people wear green!

The color stands for Ireland.

That is where this holiday is from.

My family watches a **parade** with Irish dancing.

April fools!

The first day of April is a day of jokes.

My sister has fun on April Fools Day.

It makes her laugh.

My friend loves Easter.

His family hides Easter eggs for people to find.

Some eggs are full of candy.

Yum!

On Passover, my family gets together.

We eat dinner with **special** foods.

One of those foods is matzo.

It is a very flat bread.

April 22 is Earth Day.

People get together to help the **planet**.

My family picks up **litter**.

At school, we plant a tree.

Cinco de Mayo is Spanish for the fifth of May.

People remember a **battle** that happened in Mexico long ago.

They **celebrate** being from Mexico.

Spring holidays are fun.

I love them all!

Which spring holiday do you like best?

The Story of Earth Day

The first Earth Day happened in 1970. It started in the United States to teach people about our planet.

By 1990, Earth Day had spread around the world. More people did things on this day to help the planet.

Over the years, Earth Day has grown. People keep learning about helping Earth.

Glossary

battle a fight in a war

celebrate to do special things on a certain day

litter trash that has been thrown on the ground

parade people walking together for a celebration

planet a large round object that circles the sun

special made for a certain thing

Index

April Fools Day 11
Cinco de Mayo 18
Earth Day 16, 22
Easter 12
Holi 6–7
Passover 15
St. Patrick's Day 8

Read More

Gaertner, Meg. *Earth Day (Spring Is Here)*. Lake Elmo, MN: Focus Readers, 2020.

Murray, Julie. *Spring Holidays (Seasons: Spring Cheer!)*. Minneapolis: Abdo Publishing, 2021.

Learn More Online

1. Go to **www.factsurfer.com** or scan the QR code below.
2. Enter "**Spring Holidays**" into the search box.
3. Click on the cover of this book to see a list of websites.

About the Author

J. P. Press likes books and celebrating special days.